NATIONAL GEOGRAPHIC

Now and Then

Faridah Yusof

 This is how we cook now.

This is how people used to cook.

 This is how we keep food cold now.

This is how people used to keep food cold.

 This is how we wash our clothes now.

This is how people used to wash clothes.

8 This is how we travel now.

This is how people used to travel.

 This is how we see at night now.

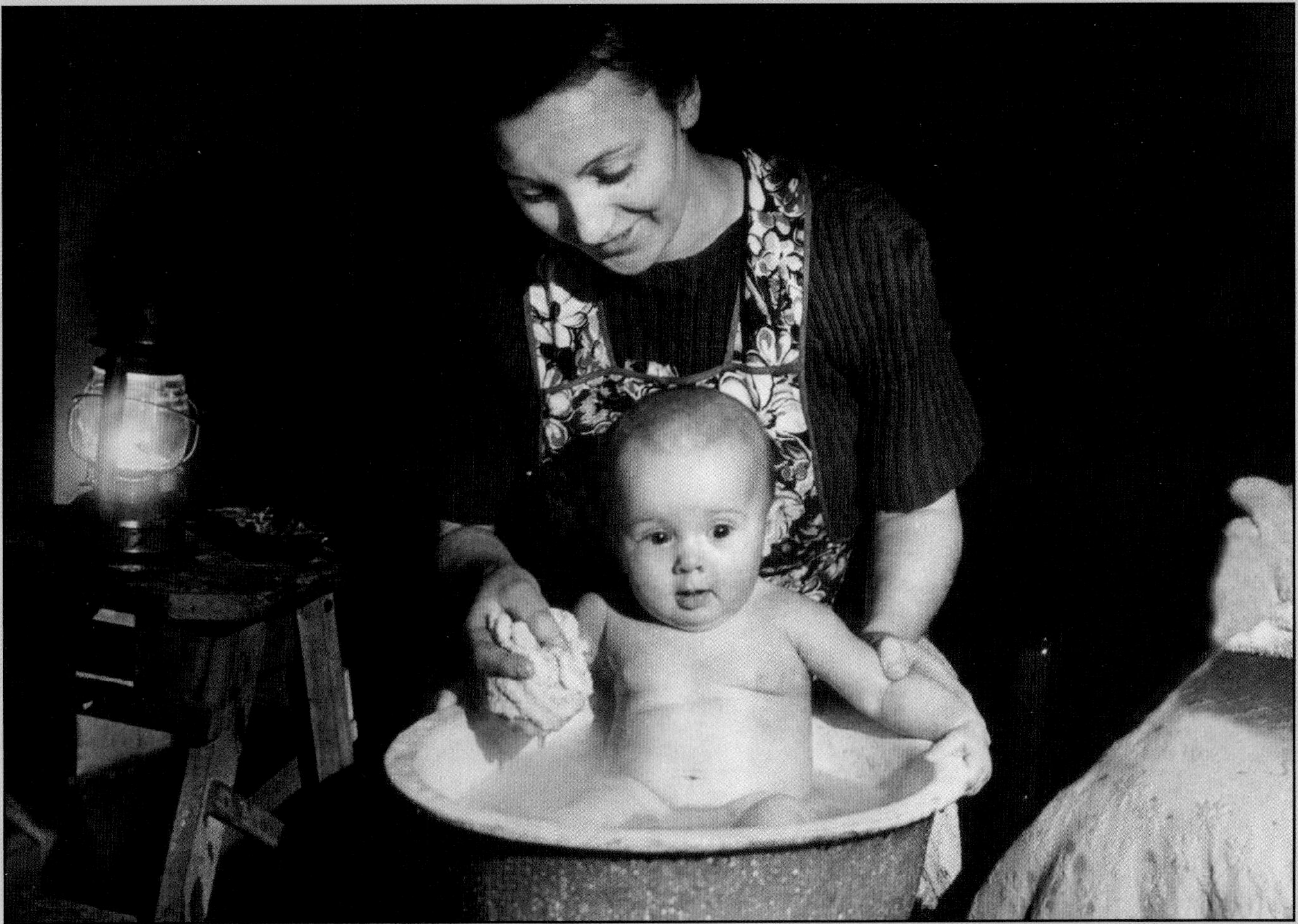

This is how people used to see at night.

Now

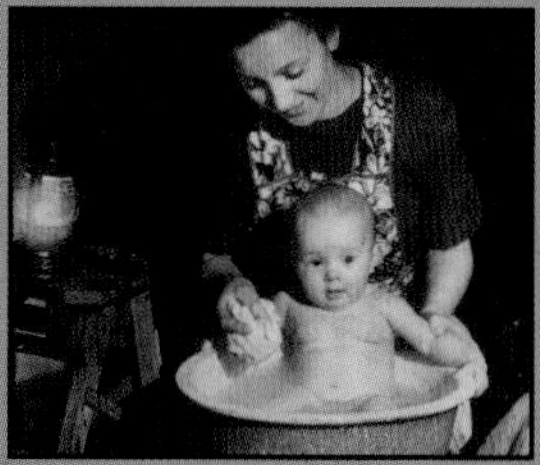

Then